PRAISE FOR *TREASURE IN THE TALES*

"*Treasure in the Tales: Finding the Gospel in Fairy Tales* is an amazing tool for parents that helps them navigate as they lay a biblical foundation for their children. The applications for each fairy tale bring clarity and hope that is deeply practical and biblically rich! With tremendous insight and experience, David takes each story and points to Christ by faith and is realistically wise, immediately applicable, and filled with insight."

—Deborah Harrell, Overseas Educational Advisor, Serge. Author, *What's Up? Elementary, Learning about Jesus and Yourself, What's Up? Discovering the Gospel, Jesus and Who You REALLY Are*, and *The Gospel Centered Parent*

"Humans have always been drawn to stories. Some stories are fictional, while other stories are true. Stories that are not true, at least the best ones, can nevertheless point us to deep truths about ourselves and about God. This book is an insightful guide, not only in revealing truths hidden in classic fairy tales, but also in inspiring us and our children to read stories with depth and imagination."

—Alexander Hartemink, Professor of Computer Science and Biology at Duke University

"In Deuteronomy 11, we are instructed to talk about the Lord with our children while we walk along the road, when we lie down, and when we get up. In the 21st century, that means we need to point our children to Christ while riding in the minivan, while reading bedtime stories, and while chatting at the breakfast table. A great tool to aid parents in this joyful but sometimes difficult duty is Dr. David Swayne's *Treasure in the Tales: Finding the Gospel in Fairy Tales.* Dr. Swayne guides Christian parents in both seeing and discussing biblically related themes from well-known fairy tales. Never will *Hansel and Gretel* be the same again! If you have children or grandchildren who are still reading and enjoying fairy tales, you should buy this book."

—Robert L. Plummer, Ph.D., Professor of New Testament Interpretation at The Southern Baptist Theological Seminary

"David Swayne's *Treasure in the Tales: Finding the Gospel in Fairy Tales* is a critical resource for the family. Each chapter is an invitation to see the beauty of the gospel as David winsomely engages familiar stories. With practical questions and real-life application, this book will encourage all who read its pages."

—Josh Kwasny, Chief Production Officer at SonicAire, Pastor at Redeemer Yadkin Valley

"Do not assume you know how to rear a child, then find out when it is too late that you did not know what you were doing. Learn from others who do it well. And here is a book from one who is good at daddying. Using the familiar to fire the child's imagination and think critically in Christ, this book is a gem of a tool for every serious parent who wants their child to understand the world biblically."

—Stephen M. Crotts, Director of the Carolina Study Center

Treasure
in the Tales

Treasure in the Tales

Finding the Gospel in Fairy Tales

David Swayne

KINDLING
·PRESS·

Published by Kindling Press, Winston-Salem, North Carolina

Edited and designed by Girl Friday Productions
www.girlfridayproductions.com

Illustrations: Lenny Wen
Design: Paul Barrett
Editorial: Alexander Rigby, Clete Smith,
Sharon Turner Mulvihill, Julie Klein

Hardcover ISBN: 978-1-7331844-0-3
Paperback ISBN: 978-1-7331844-1-0

*To parents who are endeavoring to
lead their children to the treasure*

Contents

Introduction

"OK, Dad, do one," my ten-year-old son challenged me as we were driving home from church. I had just finished saying that fairy tale stories all had a component of truth and beauty, but they also served to point toward a grander, more majestic story. On the flip side, I shared with him that these stories each contained mistruths that were not congruent with what the Bible teaches about life. I expressed to my wife, "Wouldn't it be great if someone would write a book as a primer for Christian parents to be able to emphasize the beauty and point out where the stories go sideways?" Ah, the irony of questions like this one, where the asker becomes the answer.

This book you are now holding is the outcome of attempting to answer that question!

Before we begin, let me give you a general idea of the landscape of this primer. Each chapter will start with a summary of a fairy tale (which will be worthwhile reading even if you are familiar with the tale, as there are different versions of many of these fairy tales). Following this summary, I point out what is noble and good, then discuss the not-so-commendable aspects of the tale.

The central part of each chapter highlights some facet of the radiance of the gospel. It is my intent to emphasize how each of these stories is a signpost pointing us toward an aspect of the captivating person of Jesus.

Each chapter concludes with a Scripture (English Standard Version) that I found relevant to the topic.

I then pose two sets of questions, Parental Ponderings and Kids Kickstarts, with the hope that these will help facilitate meaningful thought for parents and helpful conversation with their kids. Remember, these are just my musings: please feel free to personalize the questions for the purpose of engaging your family.

It also bears noting that these fairy tales have stood the test of time and are well loved by both the young and young at heart. The question of why these stories have so permeated the hearts and minds of generations of children begs asking. My best answer is that we each desire, long for, and even ache for many of the emphasized themes found within the tales . . . belonging, acceptance, love, happiness, justice, security, and rescue. Ultimately, however, these stories fall short of satisfying our innate, heartfelt longings, as only one Story has the power to do that.

In addition, I have attempted to structure this book thematically. The first three tales emphasize the theme of identity. The next grouping of three focuses on integrity. The third grouping highlights the concept of sacrifice. And the last grouping of fairy tales hones in on the topic of freedom. Of course, there is overlap in many of these stories, along with a number of additional themes, but I believe you will find this structure useful, especially if used as a resource for teaching.

So begins this fairy tale primer. May it help you to look at the gospel like you might look at a rare diamond . . . perhaps turning the gem ever so slightly each chapter to see a different perspective of something utterly beautiful. And may it better equip you to better equip your children with the iridescence of the gospel.

Part I

IDENTITY

Chapter One

THE UGLY DUCKLING

Let me start this chapter by encouraging you to read Hans Christian Andersen's tale *The Ugly Duckling*. Google it. In fact, stop reading this book now and read the 1844 version. I will do my best to summarize, but it truly is a striking story worth contemplating.

Essentially, this is a story about identity. Who are you? What do you believe to be true about yourself? What is your purpose?

The story begins with an egg that is larger than the others and is the very last to hatch. This last duckling is unsightly. He is rejected by his siblings and mother. The ducks peck him, the chickens beat him, and the girl who feeds the poultry kicks him. A cat mocks him, a hen calls him absurd, and eventually he even gets frozen in ice. His rescue comes in the form of a peasant, whose family frightens the duckling so much as to drive him to escape into the misery of surviving a desolate winter on his own. In addition to physical hardships, he is the constant recipient of words from others that inflict violence upon his soul:

"Yes, but he is so big and ugly."

"The others are very pretty children," said the old duck, "all but that one; I wish his mother could improve him a little."

Even his brothers and sisters are unkind to him and say, "Ah, you ugly creature, I wish the cat would get you." And his mother says she wishes he had never been born.

"You are exceedingly ugly."

Unfortunately, as the duckling is bathed in the insults of others, he begins to embrace what they are saying as he starts to insult himself:

"I will fly to those royal birds," he exclaimed, "and they will kill me, because I am so ugly."

"Kill me," said the poor bird.

By the end of the story, defeated, broken, and resigned to his ugliness, he heads toward the beautiful swans with the expectation that they will kill him. It was then that he realizes he is a swan himself.

On a positive note, the duckling in this story exhibits an amazing level of resilience and perseverance in the midst of external chaos in his life. However, toward the conclusion of the tale, it is the internal chaos in his mind that convinces him that his life is not worth continuing.

Sadly, this story resonates with life in so many ways. Who hasn't felt alone or accused or insufficient? Does anyone else hear voices of criticism? Sometimes the loudest voice is the one inside your own head.

Even now, I have many voices of doubt and condemnation in my head: *This chapter is poorly written . . . No one is going to read this book . . . Is it really worth the time I am spending?* Here's my favorite: *You are neither an author, a fairy tale writer, nor a pastor, and you have nothing of value to say.* Ouch.

Words have power to shape the way we think about ourselves and can impact our identity. If we heed the voices of criticism often enough, they will persuade us to believe things about ourselves that may not be true. So how do we respond to these voices in a healthy way? Before answering this question, we need to examine how and where we are placing our identity. As people tend to struggle with this issue in a variety of ways, I will try to put them in groups. Full disclosure: at one point or another, I have been in each one of them.

One group of people simply wants to fit in. They want other people to like them. The thought of being rejected or alone is terrifying. Because they fear being who they are, they try to copy other people. This leads them to do things they know they shouldn't do out of fear that if they don't, they won't be accepted. Fear is the main driver motivating their decisions in their life.

Another group of people finds their identity in what they do. Let's say it's their job, and they're fired. It leads to despair, hopelessness, and depression. Many find themselves in counseling or on medication to treat their symptoms. They have been rejected by the very thing that gave them their identity, and it is devastating.

Another group of people cares only about themselves. They do what they want, when they want. The ramifications of their actions on others are of no relevance, because life (from their perspective) revolves around them. Their lives are marked by sadness as they find themselves alone without any true friends.

To make it clear, the Bible says we are sinners and fall far short of perfection. If that were where the gospel story ended, we would have every reason to be without hope!

In the gospel story, however, we see another kind of Ugly Duckling. This one came after many prophets hatched before him. He was born amid the foul smells of animals and the filth of a manger. His siblings rejected him. His parents left him behind in a temple. His friends betrayed him. He was mocked, beaten, and abused. The Bible describes him as "despised and rejected by men, a man of sorrows and acquainted with grief; and as one from whom men hide their faces." (Isaiah 53:3) Unlike the duck in the tale, Jesus was brutally killed. On the cross, he suffered far beyond the mere pain of physical death. Spiritually, he became the definition of ugly when he bore the weight of our sin. Why would he do this?

Love. Jesus' depth of love runs deeper than I can fathom. He wanted to rescue us from the foolishness of a wasted life and welcome us into his better plan for our lives.

This beautiful Savior came to die for us so that we would be freed from the bondage of fear and awakened to the reality that we are deeply loved. The Bible uses a beautiful word to describe God's chosen ones: "beloved" (Colossians 3:12). To be beloved means that, without a shadow of a doubt, you are deeply and dearly loved. And so he invites us to listen to his voice beckoning, "Beloved." Do you hear him? Listen again: "Beloved. Chosen one. Forgiven." Let his identity-defining words of affirmation drown out every voice of criticism in your head.

And when the inevitable accusations—quite opposite to words like "beloved"—fill our minds, remember instead what the gospel tells us. The word "gospel" literally means good news, which I think may be one of the greatest understatements of the word "good" in the history of its usage! It truly is phenomenal news to consider that we could benefit from the sacrificial life, death, and resurrection of Jesus. His loving rescue of people like you and me (who fall far short of the perfect life that only Jesus could live) necessitates a response. If by faith we accept not only his rescue of us but also his loving lordship over our lives, the absolutely amazing, mind-boggling, inexplicable outcome is that Jesus in turn gives us his beauty, his rightness, and his identity. Our identity is now defined by the value Jesus has given us. In addition, we are also promised that he will never leave us, that there is purpose in suffering (even if we do not understand it), and that one day all things will be restored and made right.

That helps me when I get schizophrenic going from one confused identity to another. It frees me from craving the accolades and acceptance of others and shields me from their criticism, because those words no longer define me. I don't spiral into hopelessness when I lose my job, because it does not define who I am and ultimately has never been my provider. And I am free from the sorrowful delusion that life is all about me.

In sum, I have been liberated to give my life away for the benefit of others BECAUSE Jesus gave his life away for my benefit.

So, knowing this, what shall I say to the voices of criticism in my own head about this chapter? I would say that because I have been loved much, to the degree that I am able to express my understanding of how beautiful Jesus is in the context of this book for your benefit, it is worth my care, thoughts, and time.

Lastly, by way of application, if you have a preteen, tell them that Jesus loves them. He is the most beautiful swan, who became an ugly duckling because he wanted us to be beautiful swans too.

If you have a teenager, ask them about their identity. How important is it for them to fit in with their peer group? What identity group would they say that they fall into? I promise you, this is absolutely relevant for them right now.

May your children more frequently hear words of affirmation from you than criticism. And may you have the grace to lovingly engage them with the most precious Ugly Duckling humanity has ever known.

Looking to Jesus, the founder and perfecter of our faith, who for the joy that was set before him endured the cross, despising the shame, and is seated at the right hand of the throne of God.
—Hebrews 12:2

PARENTAL PONDERINGS

Which do you do more frequently: speak words of encouragement and affirmation to your children/spouse or speak words of criticism? When was the last time your children/spouse heard you say to them "I was wrong for _____. Will you forgive me?"

KIDS KICKSTARTS

When was the last time someone said something mean to you? How did it make you feel? How does knowing that you are loved by Jesus help?

Chapter Two

SNOW WHITE AND THE SEVEN DWARFS

In the story of Snow White, we are confronted with the tension between good and evil.

Snow White is unknowingly the object of her stepmother's jealousy. The stepmother has been the most beautiful woman in the world, and one day her magic mirror tells her that Snow White is now the fairest of them all. Driven by rage and jealousy, she seeks to eliminate her enemy by commanding a huntsman to take Snow White into the forest and cut out her heart. Fortunately for Snow White, the huntsman releases her and brings the wicked queen the heart of a boar instead. Snow White wanders through the forest until she meets up with the seven dwarfs in their house. They allow her to stay as long as she prepares food for them and cleans their clothes. Once the magic mirror reveals that Snow White is still alive, the stepmother disguises herself as an old woman and brings her a magical poisoned apple to eat. When Snow White takes a bite, she falls down dead and is placed in a glass coffin. Eventually a prince sees her and is so enamored with her beauty that he just wants to look at her the rest of his life—even though she is dead. In the original tale by the Brothers Grimm, the people carrying the coffin for the prince stumble, causing the poison apple to dislodge from her throat, and she awakens. In the more recent version, it is the kiss of the prince that awakens her. It is love at first sight—they marry and live happily ever after.

There is much to say about this story. On the positive side, there is the kindness and bravery of the huntsman, who chooses not to kill Snow White at the peril of his own life. There is the servant's attitude that Snow White exhibits in her willingness to care for seven dwarfs she has never met before. There is the hope that when all seems lost after eating the poisoned apple, the possibility of a restored life and happiness yet remain.

More concerning to me are the prominent negative seeds that this fairy tale may plant in the hearts of our kids. The focus is so clearly on the physical beauty of Snow White. So compelling is her beauty that it drives one woman mad with rage and another man to propose marriage on sight!

This emphasis on physical beauty is so pervasive in our culture. Women are compelled to look a certain way to fit in or risk feeling ostracized if they don't. Objectification of women has become "normalized" by the pervasive accessibility of pornography. It is a deeply troubling cultural norm that women should be devalued and demeaned in ways that are intended to create profit from the lustful eyes of others.

As a counterbalance, there is nothing wrong with physical beauty, and it is a positive thing that the prince was attracted to Snow White. Oh, but beauty is so much more than skin-deep; just look at how ugly the jealous rage made the stepmother.

What I would like you to share with your kids is that women are beautiful not just in their physical attributes but more so in their inner beauty—their passions, hopes, joys, character, actions; the books they love, friends they cherish, words they say, and things they do. We want their identity to be confidently connected to their integrity, not insecurely dependent upon others' perceptions of their appearance.

Young men should be taught to respect women. To be considerate and kind. To foster friendship as the foundation of a relationship. To not expect (as this fairy tale implies) that love happens at first sight. To turn away from demeaning images and courageously stand up for dignity. Our kids should be encouraged to consider the interests of the other gender to be at least as important as their own. I think if we promote these ideas and plant these seeds into the minds and hearts of our kids, their future marriages (if that is God's plan for them) will have a much greater potential for real relationship, sacrificial love, and joy of friendship amid the inevitable travails of life together.

And how about the gospel? Where do we find that in *Snow White*? Remember that there was a poisonous fruit of sorts in the Garden of Eden. Like the stepmother, there was a deceiving snake who persuaded

Eve to eat the forbidden fruit. And while this did not (initially) lead to physical death, it immediately led to spiritual death. Adam and Eve, because of their sin, died (fell asleep) spiritually and were separated from their relationship with the God who loved them and created them. From that time on, all of us have been separated from God because of sin. But there is a beautiful Prince of Peace who purchased this peace by giving his life as a sacrifice of love. This Savior willingly ate the whole poisonous apple of sin so that what we had already eaten would not leave us dead forever.

In Jesus' death on the cross, God's justice and mercy met in a kiss. Don't miss this, friends! God's justice required that there be punishment for sin, and at the same time, God's mercy yearned to restore us to a right relationship with him. These two seemingly opposed attributes were brought together and reconciled at the cross. In love, mercy and justice met with the intimacy of a kiss. Have you felt the life-giving kiss of the Prince? If we believe this and turn away from sin (repent), God gives us his Spirit. The poison of the apple loses its grip on us. We awaken from our spiritual slumber to restored life, union with Christ, and purpose to serve him with gratitude for the remainder of our days. Hallelujah! Tell that story to your kids!

> *Charm is deceitful, and beauty is vain, but a woman who fears the LORD is to be praised.*
> —*Proverbs 31:30*

PARENTAL PONDERINGS

In what ways have you witnessed the perversion of physical beauty by our culture? How do you try to live counterculturally on this issue?

KIDS KICKSTARTS

Have you ever been made fun of for how you look? How did that make you feel? How does knowing that Jesus loves the entirety of who you are right now make you feel? Would you rather have someone love you for how you look or for who you are?

Chapter Three

PINOCCHIO

In the story of Pinocchio, we are introduced to a lump of wood that makes a moaning noise when chipped. This lump of wood is so unusual that it is rejected by a carpenter, who gives it to a cobbler named Geppetto. Geppetto wants to make a puppet and carves out the head, hair, eyes, nose, legs, and hands. Of course, Pinocchio's nose keeps growing longer, and no matter how often Geppetto tries to cut it short, it just grows long again. The story tells us that as Pinocchio is being made, he sticks his tongue out at Geppetto, grabs his wig, and kicks him, causing the old man's eyes to brim with tears. Geppetto then teaches Pinocchio to walk, and immediately thereafter Pinocchio runs away from home. When Pinocchio is brought home by the police, Geppetto kindly makes Pinocchio a suit, shoes, and a hat.

Pinocchio then wants to go to school, but he never makes it there as he is distracted by a puppet show. The puppet master, Giovanni, who adds Pinocchio to the show, is cruel to the puppets. When his meal is undercooked, he demands that a puppet be used as firewood so that it can be properly cooked. Pinocchio volunteers to be burned instead of another puppet, which moves the heart of the puppet master so much that he decides to eat the meal as it is. Furthermore, after hearing more of Pinocchio's story, Giovanni decides to give Pinocchio five gold coins and to let him go.

On his way home, Pinocchio meets a half-blind cat and a lame fox. They trick Pinocchio and steal his money. Pinocchio then gets assaulted and is rescued by a fairy, who provides him with medicine and care. When he lies to the fairy, his nose grows; she corrects him, has woodpeckers restore his nose to normal length, and advises him to lie no more. She then gives him some money and lets him go home to Geppetto.

Geppetto welcomes him and gets him set to go to school once more. But his path gets diverted again by a friend who convinces him to go to a magical place called Toyland. As the days pass, the boys begin to be transformed into donkeys. Pinocchio gets sold, goes lame, and is thrown to the bottom of the sea, where he cries out to the fairy for help. The fairy responds by transforming him back into his wooden self.

After reaching the surface, he flees from the man who tried to drown him by swimming out to sea. Unfortunately, his plight subsequently worsens as a shark with a "cavernlike mouth" chases and then swallows him. Inside the stomach of the shark, he finds Geppetto, who says that after searching for Pinocchio on land, he got in a boat to look for him in the sea and was also swallowed whole. Fortunately for them, the shark has asthma and sleeps with its mouth open, allowing them to escape.

They make their way home, and Pinocchio begins to work to make money. When he hears that the fairy is sick, instead of using his money on himself, he sends her some of his money to pay for her treatment. She is so touched by his kindness that, to reward him, she turns him into a real boy. The story concludes with Geppetto saying, "When bad boys become good, their looks change along with their lives!"

If you made it through that long summary, here is the reward: this story points beautifully toward the power that is able to transform your life into a new creation.

Let's start with what is good. Geppetto exhibits remarkable generosity in his willingness to forgive Pinocchio again and again. Despite the rejection, disobedience, and disrespect Pinocchio initially offers his creator, Geppetto responds in love by pursuing Pinocchio across land and sea at risk to his own life. In addition, we are presented with the hope that even a self-centered character like Pinocchio can eventually be changed into a benevolent person like Geppetto. I believe that the most important aspect of this tale, however, is understanding the role of the fairy, as I believe her to be very clearly symbolic of the Holy Spirit.

As best as I am able, I want to teach you what I know about and have experienced with the Holy Spirit. My hope is, through answering a few questions, to help you to more effectively explain the Person of the Holy Spirit to your children.

First, who is the Holy Spirit?

The Holy Spirit is a person: a "he," not an "it"; relational. Scripture reveals that the Holy Spirit speaks, acts, teaches, and expresses emotions. He relates to us in a personal way. He is holy: worthy of worship, honor, and praise. He is a Spirit: we can't see him but can see and feel his effects. Take, for example, the wind as it affects the movement of a leaf falling to the ground from a tree. We can't see the wind, but it nonetheless has a powerful effect on the leaf. Similarly, we can't see the Holy Spirit, but his effect on the life of a Christian transforms the trajectory of that person's life.

What does the Holy Spirit do?

He helps us in times of need (which, by the way, is always!).

He comforts us in times of suffering.

He convicts us of sin . . . allowing for rescue and redemption to occur.

He gives us good gifts, such as love, joy, peace, patience, kindness, goodness, faithfulness, gentleness, and self-control.

What is the connection between becoming a Christian and the Holy Spirit?

The Bible says that "if you confess with your mouth that Jesus is Lord and believe in your heart that God raised him from the dead, you will be saved." (Romans 10:9) This gift of salvation also comes with a promise, that we are given the Holy Spirit: "And Peter said to them, 'Repent and be baptized every one of you in the name of Jesus Christ for the forgiveness of your sins, and you will receive the gift of the Holy Spirit.'" (Acts 2:38)

One of the most effective ways to tell your kids about the Holy Spirit is sharing your own story of salvation. Whether you grew up in a Christian home where there was never a day that you did not know Jesus as your Savior, or were a persecutor like Saul, who met Jesus on a road to Damascus, we all have amazing stories of salvation, because it is about what Jesus has accomplished for us and the price he paid for the sins we committed. All of our stories are amazing stories of rescue, because the egregious magnitude of our sin is the same, and the focal point of all of our stories is our great Rescuer: Jesus.

What's your story?

I first believed and confessed the above verses to be true when I was around ten years old. At that time, I was given a deposit of the Holy Spirit. It's like I was a glass of milk and God poured in a large dollop of chocolate syrup that settled at the bottom of the glass. The syrup was in there, and there was no removing it.

However, my life didn't actually look too much different for the next eight years. It was not until I was in college and I heard the gospel message in a particularly compelling way that God used his "spiritual stirring spoon" to thoroughly mix the chocolate sauce through the entirety of my glass. This is how I would explain being filled with the Holy Spirit to your children. God's timing is not the same with all Christians. Sometimes, the deposit of the Holy Spirit is stirred into the milk right away, and sometimes this stirring occurs much later.

What does it mean when people talk about being born again?

The Bible also talks about being born again. Perhaps you're familiar with the story of Nicodemus. Jesus tells him that he needs to be born again of the Spirit. Think of it this way: when you were developing in your mother's womb, everything was dark. You were alive, but sounds from the outside were muffled at best, you could not see clearly, and your intellect was somewhat underdeveloped! In a similar way, before you have the Holy Spirit, you may be able to see spiritual things happen, but you cannot appropriately interpret them. You may be able to hear the effects of God, but not understand them. However, when you have the Holy Spirit, it's like God puts spiritual contact lenses in your eyes so that you will be able to interpret life through the lens of the gospel. He puts spiritual hearing aids in your ears so that words preached at church are transformative to your life. And it's like he gives you your own translator so that you can begin to understand things of a spiritual nature, whereas previously it might have been like listening to a foreign language.

In my life, as above, this occurred during college. And it was during that season of my life that I recommitted my life to Jesus. It was as if God put a pair of glasses on my eyes as everything in my life took on new meaning. Everything had purpose. Nothing was accidental.

In addition, my identity changed. I no longer defined myself as a college student but rather as a Christian who happened to be in college. My life was defined by who God said I was and by what God had done for me, not by what I did nor by what I had done for myself. As the Scripture states in 2 Corinthians 5:17, "if anyone is in Christ, he is a new creation." In other words, because of my union with Christ, I was now a child of God. 1 John 3:2 states this quite succinctly: "Beloved, we are God's children now." Understanding my born-again identity in this way has transformed the way I have lived my life.

What's the most effective way to explain the Holy Spirit to your kids?

I like the chocolate milk example, but there is one that I like more. It's the example of sleep. When we are asleep, it's kind of like being dead: we are unable to hear, move, think, see, or speak (at least not coherently!). From a spiritual standpoint, however, that is exactly the state in which we find ourselves. The Bible says that we are dead in our trespasses. When we become Christians, we are infused with life. From a spiritual standpoint, we go from dead to alive. We are awakened from our slumber of death. It's analogous to waking up: you can now think, talk, see, hear, understand, and remember. So too does the Holy Spirit help the Christian apply the gospel to the gift of each day of their life. Each day now has purpose: to live a life of gratitude toward the one who has rescued you.

OK, back to the fairy in *Pinocchio*. She exhibits many traits of the Holy Spirit, doesn't she? She helps Pinocchio in his time of need. She confronts and convicts him of his sin when she points out that his nose grows longer every time he lies. She rescues him from drowning. She strips away the donkey (symbolic of his rebellion and sin) covering his body. And she ultimately transforms him from something perishable (wood without a soul) into someone imperishable (a boy with a heart).

If this transformation from wood into flesh strikes you as familiar, it did for me as well. Remember what God said to his people in the book of Ezekiel? "And I will give you a new heart, and a new spirit I will put within you. And I will remove the heart of stone from your flesh and give you a heart of flesh. And I will put my Spirit within you, and cause you to walk in my statutes and be careful to obey my rules." (Ezekiel 36:26–27)

Friends, do you see it now? The tale of Pinocchio is another story about you and me and our need of rescue. We are all so much like Pinocchio. Loved creations who fight and kick and lie and run and disobey. Pursued by a Father who loves us and would spare nothing to secure our rescue. It would seem to be enough that Jesus would die in our place so that we might live. But God does even more. He gives us his Holy Spirit to live in us, and in doing so transforms us from wood into adopted sons and daughters of the King of Creation.

May the story of Pinocchio remind you of who you were and evoke you to worship as you remember the ongoing transformative work of the Holy Spirit in your life.

Do you not know that you are God's temple and that God's Spirit dwells in you? If anyone destroys God's temple, God will destroy him. For God's temple is holy, and you are that temple.

—1 Corinthians 3:16–17

PARENTAL PONDERINGS

When were you spiritually resurrected (what's your story of salvation)? Have you told your kids? How do you explain the Holy Spirit to your children?

KIDS KICKSTARTS

How are you like Pinocchio? Have you ever been in need of rescue? What happened? How has the Holy Spirit helped, comforted, or convicted you recently?

Part II

INTEGRITY

Chapter Four

THE THREE LITTLE PIGS

In the story of the Three Little Pigs, each pig is given the opportunity to build a house. Two of them build their homes quickly out of straw and sticks. Those two pigs then have plenty of time to have a party. The third pig, however, builds his house out of bricks. Along comes a wolf, who huffs and puffs and blows down the first two flimsily constructed homes. The pigs flee to the brick house. Try though he might, the wolf is unable to blow down the brick house. He attempts to gain entry by climbing down the chimney but ends up getting cooked to death in a pot of boiling water. The first two pigs then build their own brick houses and live happily ever after.

We see in these pigs' tale much about wisdom and folly. In life, there are daily choices regarding taking shortcuts or doing a job well. In this story, the first two pigs are described as lazy. They get their work done quickly and do not have a strong foundation for their home. The eventual ramifications for them could cost them their very lives (in fact, in some versions of the story, the wolf indeed eats the first two pigs). The third pig, by diligently building a secure house, is able to become a haven to rescue his family. As silly as it may sound, this pig exhibits integrity: he does the right thing in a reliable way.

So how does that apply to us and our kids? When we start a task, do we do it completely or just partway? By way of example (and also confession), I will share a story from my youth. When I was a child, we used ice trays to make ice (no built-in ice maker back then!). I loved ice in my drinks and used to empty the tray down to one last cube, then put it back in the freezer. Whoever used the last cube of ice in any given tray would have to fill the ice tray back up with water. I could hold out for weeks until someone else used the last cube and filled up the tray. Man, what a reflection of the self-centered nature of my heart . . . sorry, Mom!

How about other examples: Kids, do you help put the family's dirty dishes into the dishwasher . . . or do you just leave them all in the sink for someone else to do? Students, do you rush through your schoolwork in order to get to something you'd rather do? Ever been tempted to cheat? Ever cheated? Dads, do you move the chairs out from under the table when vacuuming or just slide the vacuum in and out as quick as you can? Parents, do you take the time to engage the condition of your child's heart when disobedience occurs, or do you just look for the behavioral fix? I am sure you have your own list of convicting questions penetrating your mind right now. The bottom line is this: what kind of a house are you trying to build every day?

The Bible has a really fantastic verse to address this question. "Unless the LORD builds the house, those who build it labor in vain." (Psalm 127:1)

In case you are beginning to feel inept or guilty, now is a great time to remind you of the grace seen in this story. Remember, we are ALL like the first two pigs. We all have need to repent and to be rescued. Isn't it wonderful and reassuring to know that our God is a God of second chances? He gives us grace upon grace even as we continue to try to construct homes of straw and stick. And ultimately, he builds us a better home. In Jesus, we have someone who has done just that— built an indestructible, eternal brick home.

In addition (incredulously, to my mind!), the Bible says that Jesus himself has prepared a room for us in this home.

"In my Father's house are many rooms. If it were not so, would I have told you that I go to prepare a place for you? And if I go and prepare a place for you, I will come again and will take you to myself, that where I am you may be also." (John 14:2–3)

Is that reminder not the best thing you've heard all day? YOU GET A ROOM IN JESUS' HOUSE! That is crazy amazing. He will take us there and be with us there. There may well be storms in our lives, our homes of sticks and straw may be blown over, but we have a promise of rescue from one who will never break his word.

Furthermore, we are invited into the beautiful work of the home he has prepared for us. "As you come to him, a living stone rejected by men but in the sight of God chosen and precious, you yourselves like living stones are being built up as a spiritual house, to be a holy priesthood, to offer spiritual sacrifices acceptable to God through Jesus Christ." (1 Peter 2:4–5)

To summarize: Jesus has built the house of refuge. We get a room! He invites us to join the work of the advancement of his kingdom as a "living brick" in his house.

So where is the gospel in the story? The good news of the gospel is that Jesus was willing to leave his home to come to Earth. He was born amid the sticks and straw of a manger. He was pursued by the worst wolf ever, the devil. He traveled the earth as a vagabond with no place to rest his head . . . worse off than a fox, a bird, or a pig (Matthew 8:20). He was misunderstood, mocked, and maligned. There was no sibling with a brick house. There was no rescue. Unlike in the tale of the Three Little Pigs, the devil isn't killed in the pot of boiling water. Jesus is. He dives in because his perfect love is more powerful than death. Amazingly, this was all by design. Preplanned. Jesus was on a mission to die for us so that we might be rescued. He purposefully laid down his life on the cross so that our sins would not cause us to perish before a holy God.

Seemingly paradoxically, it was his death on the cross that actually secured for us a place in his inde-structible home. The Bible says that, through his death, Jesus destroyed "the one who has the power of death, that is, the devil." (Hebrews 2:14) This is astounding to me. Jesus' death defeated the devil's power. Because Jesus rose from the grave proving his power over death, the offer on hand for us is that if we trust in him as our Rescuer and ask him to forgive us, he does. We are adopted into his family as daughters and sons, and we become living bricks in his house who have the privilege of serving him with gratitude for the duration of our days on earth and for all eternity with him. That sounds more like the "living happily ever after" that I want!

The LORD is good, a stronghold in the day of trouble; he knows those who take refuge in him.
                                                    —*Nahum 1:7*

PARENTAL PONDERINGS

Which materials are you currently using to build your house . . . straw, stick, or brick? How does knowing what Jesus has accomplished encourage you to build your house in a different way? Do you have any "ice cube" stories your family would enjoy hearing about?

KIDS KICKSTARTS

What are some ways that you have taken shortcuts in your life? What was the outcome? How does understanding how much Jesus loves you help you want to do things the right way?

Chapter Five

JACK AND THE BEANSTALK

In the last fairy tale, *The Three Little Pigs*, we saw an example of a pig that was trustworthy and reliable, and this led to the rescue of his family. In the story of Jack and the Beanstalk, we are introduced to a main character in whom we would be hard-pressed to find traces of integrity. In fact, he may well be close to the exact opposite of the character traits we would like to instill in our children! Having said that, let's proceed with a refresher on this tale.

The story begins by introducing us to a poor widow and her son, Jack. Because of their abject poverty, his mother tells Jack to sell their only cow. Jack goes to the market and sells the cow to a man for five magic beans. When he comes home, his mother is furious and says, "You fool." She throws the beans out the window and sends Jack to bed without dinner. Upon awakening the next day, Jack finds a huge beanstalk has grown. He climbs it to reach a kingdom in the sky, where he finds the home of a giant and his wife. Jack goes inside their house and finds the wife in the kitchen. Emboldened by his hunger, he asks her for some food, and she kindly offers him bread and milk. While he is eating, the giant returns home. Jack is terrified and hides. The giant wants to eat him, famously exclaiming, "Fee-fi-fo-fum, I smell the blood of an Englishman." The wife protects Jack and convinces the giant that there is no boy in their home. When the giant eventually falls asleep, Jack creeps out of his hiding place, steals one sack of gold coins, and climbs down the beanstalk. A few days later, Jack climbs back up, and the same scenario happens. This time, however, the giant takes out his hen, which proceeds to lay a golden egg. When the giant falls asleep, Jack steals the hen and climbs down the beanstalk. After another couple of days, Jack once again climbs the beanstalk in search of more treasure to plunder. In contrast to Jack's dishonesty, the wife persists in her kindness by providing him with more food and protecting him from her flesh-eating husband. This time, Jack sees the giant's magical harp that can play beautiful songs. When the giant falls asleep, Jack steals the harp and is about to leave, but suddenly the magic harp cries, "Help, master! A boy is stealing me!" The giant wakes up and runs after Jack. Jack hurries down the beanstalk with the giant in close pursuit. Jack gets his ax, chops down the beanstalk, and the giant falls to his death. The story concludes by telling us that Jack and his mother are now very rich and live happily ever after.

To be clear, there's not much beauty to be found within the story. At best, there is the benevolence exhibited multiple times by the wife to feed Jack and not turn him over to her husband, who would eat him. And that's about it.

The rest of the story seems to be about a foolish boy who sells their cow for magic beans. He then repays the kindness of a woman who feeds him by stealing her gold, precious hen, and magical harp. Hardly commendable behavior! Finally, he commits murder to protect his plunder, leaving the giant's wife a widow.

So perhaps the moral of the story is to be foolish, take advantage of people, steal from them (multiple times), and commit murder in order to live a better life. Hmm . . . just maybe not the exact message I'd like to convey to my children!

Although Jack is clearly not the role model that I would have my children emulate, I am reminded that there are stories from my own life that are similarly deceptive. Take, for example, the point at which my brother and I were old enough to stay home alone without a babysitter. The rule of the house was no throwing balls inside the house. Of course, what was one of the things we did first when my parents would go out? Play catch inside with a Nerf football! One evening when we were doing this, my brother hit a teacup on a side table, causing it to fall and shatter. We decided to replace it with a regular cup from the kitchen cabinet. We didn't learn our lesson and kept playing that night, and one of my errant throws subsequently took out a fancy display plate on a mantel above the fireplace. Exhibiting similar brilliance, we decided to replace it with a regular dinner plate. As you can imagine, it did not take long for our deception to be discovered, and as I recall, the consequences were not particularly pleasant.

The Bible tells lots of stories about people who disobey and deceive; it's one of many reasons I think there's hope for me! One story in particular has some really interesting similarities to *Jack and the Beanstalk*. It's a story about another deceiver named Jacob.

For the first similarity, we need not go further than the name Jack. Jack is thought to be derived from Jacques, the French form of the name Jacob. It is my strong suspicion that it was no accident that the author of this fairy tale chose the name Jack for the intended purpose of directing readers to the biblical story of Jacob. Remember, Jacob tricked his brother Esau into selling Esau's birthright for bread and a bowl of stew. Later, Jacob also tricked his father into giving Jacob his blessing (which by order of birth belonged to his older brother Esau). If Jacob could have stolen a golden egg-laying hen, I bet he would have!

The next similarity we find is in the parallel between the fairy tale and the biblical narrative regarding Jacob's dream. Take a moment and read what Scripture says about this dream:

> "And he dreamed, and behold, there was a ladder set up on the earth, and the top of it reached to heaven. And behold, the angels of God were ascending and descending on it! And behold, the LORD stood above it and said, 'I am the LORD, the God of Abraham your father and the God of Isaac. The land on which you lie I will give to you and to your offspring. Your

offspring shall be like the dust of the earth, and you shall spread abroad to the west and to the east and to the north and to the south, and in you and your offspring shall all the families of the earth be blessed. Behold, I am with you and will keep you wherever you go, and will bring you back to this land. For I will not leave you until I have done what I have promised you.'

Then Jacob awoke from his sleep and said, 'Surely the LORD is in this place, and I did not know it.' And he was afraid and said, 'How awesome is this place! This is none other than the house of God, and this is the gate of heaven.'" —Genesis 28:12–17

In this dream, we find God the Father at the top of a ladder telling Jacob that he would be with him, multiply his family, and never leave him. We are told that this ladder is set up on Earth and reaches to heaven. Sounds a little like a beanstalk, right? Oh friends, hang on, this is where it gets exciting!

Look at what Jesus says about this passage when he talks with Nathaniel (who he describes as an Israelite with no deceit, alluding to Jacob): "And he said to him, 'Truly, truly, I say to you, you will see heaven opened, and the angels of God ascending and descending on the Son of Man.'" (John 1:51)

Do you see it? This is so fantastically cool! Jesus is referring to Jacob's dream in this passage. In Jacob's dream, the angels are ascending and descending on the ladder. In Jesus' statement, they are ascending and descending on the Son of Man, which is a reference to himself. Jesus is in clear terms saying that he is the ladder in Jacob's dream.

Jesus is the ladder bridging the gap between an Earth full of messed-up people like Jack, Jacob, you, and me, and a perfectly holy, just, and loving Father. We can live our lives trying to climb this ladder to reach heaven based on our efforts, only to live a life of exhaustion not even climbing one rung. Or by faith, we can rest on the perfect performance of Jesus, who came down from heaven to Earth to live the life we could not live, die the death we deserved to die, credit us with righteousness we did not earn, and bring us up this ladder to heaven where we are given "an inheritance that is imperishable, undefiled, and unfading." (1 Peter 1:4) Wow.

You see, Jesus is not only the ladder, but he is the one who climbs the ladder with us literally strapped to his back. He climbs this ladder rung by rung as he bears the brunt of the wounds received while living on Earth, endures the shame of the cross, defeats death through the resurrection, and ascends to heaven. And when he stands before the Father in heaven, because of his unblemished record, he presents you similarly unblemished alongside him. Jesus has removed all your guilt, shame, and sin, presenting you with a smile on his face, saying, "Look Dad, I got one . . . I rescued this one! I brought her with me up my ladder. This is my sister. This is your daughter." To which the Father replies, "Well done, my good and faithful children." The angels rejoice, there is singing resounding in heaven, and a feast is laid out before you. Amazing grace.

OK, here is one last comparison. In *Jack and the Beanstalk,* Jack fearfully chops down the beanstalk, and in doing so, kills the giant to temporarily keep the treasures he has stolen. In the gospel story, however, Jesus purposefully allows his life to be cut down to give us a permanent treasure that we cannot earn, deserve, or lose.

The apostle Paul describes it this way: "For you know the grace of our Lord Jesus Christ, that though he was rich, yet for your sake he became poor, so that you by his poverty might become rich." (2 Corinthians 8:9)

May the amazing generosity of Jesus to you melt your heart freshly today. May you know the riches that he offers, the rescue he has accomplished, and the hope he has secured for you through his death and resurrection. And by his Spirit, may you be transformed into a person of integrity who looks a lot less like Jack and a lot more like Jesus.

Blessed be the God and Father of our Lord Jesus Christ! According to his great mercy, he has caused us to be born again to a living hope through the resurrection of Jesus Christ from the dead, to an inheritance that is imperishable, undefiled, and unfading, kept in heaven for you.

—1 Peter 1:3–4

PARENTAL PONDERINGS

Do you have any Nerf football stories of disobedience from your youth? Have you shared these stories with your family? In your life, would you say that you are more often trying to climb the ladder on your own strength, or resting on the grace that is sufficient for you?

KIDS KICKSTARTS

If you were Jack, would you have taken the hen with the golden eggs? Why or why not? If you were the giant's wife, would you have treated Jack as she did? If everyone on earth acted like Jack did, do you think that Jesus would still have come to die for us?

Chapter Six

LITTLE RED RIDING HOOD

In *Little Red Riding Hood,* we find a girl sent on an errand by her mother to bring food and wine to her grandmother. She has to go through the woods to get to the house and is told by her mother to stay on the path.

On the way, the girl gets distracted by some flowers and deviates from the path. A hungry wolf sees her and joins her along the journey. The wolf then goes ahead, eats the grandmother, puts on the grandmother's clothes, and gets in bed.

When the girl arrives, she exclaims, "How big your eyes are, Grandma," and "How sharp your teeth are!" The wolf then eats her whole as well. In the commotion, a woodcutter comes to the rescue and uses his ax to cut both her and her grandma out of the belly of the wolf.

Wow, now that's a scary children's story if I ever heard one!

On a positive note, I think the actions of the wood-cutter clearly highlight the good in this tale. It took incredible courage and kindness to enter the fray and risk his life to engage the wolf on behalf of people he may not have even known. Impressive.

Truth be told, however, aren't we all much more frequently like Little Red than the heroic woodcut-ter? Who among us has not strayed from the path of obedience? Who among us has not felt the gnawing consequences of sin? Has anyone else ever avoided conflict rather than engage it with the purpose of ben-efitting the other person? Which leads to questions of larger significance: Why should a perfect and holy God accept people who have not lived up to his standards? How can one be rescued not only from death but also from being judged as deserving punishment for our sins?

In addition to these troubling questions, there really is a wolf—the devil. Just like the wolf wearing the grandmother's clothes, the devil used to be an angel but was thrown out of heaven when he decided he wanted to be in control. He is even now described in the Bible as disguising himself as an angel of light (2 Corinthians 11:14) and prowling around like a roar-ing lion seeking someone to devour (1 Peter 5:8). So we find ourselves in a MUCH worse predicament than Little Red; we face a more horrific enemy and, after death, a perfect judge. We need someone much more capable than a man with an ax to rescue us . . . we need a miracle. To top it off, the devil thought that he had his greatest victory when Jesus was killed on the cross. Game over, right?

But Jesus was very different from Little Red. You see, Jesus did what we and Little Red could not. He did EVERYTHING right. Jesus was completely obedient to everything that his Father asked him to do. Jesus never strayed from the path, no matter the temptations that were placed in his way by the devil. Jesus was on a mission of love for you as he walked this path of righteousness directly to the cross. I think that bears repeating: Jesus was on a mission of love for you. He knew that we (you and I) had no chance against the wolf. Because of our mistakes in life (our sins), we would have no chance against the power of death, and in the subsequent accounting we would give to a holy God, we would be judged unacceptable to live with him for eternity.

Jesus, however, did not need a woodcutter to escape the belly of death. When Jesus died on the cross, the grave did not hold any power over him. Jesus had lived the life we could not: perfect in every way. When he died on the cross, he died as a sacrifice for us, taking the punishment we deserved. When he rose from the grave on Easter, he proved his power over death and the certainty of his ability to rescue us.

The offer on hand is that if we ask the Father to forgive us and accept Jesus as our great Woodcutter (Lord and Savior), we begin a personal relationship with him now, and then we will be welcomed into heaven for eternity. A great exchange occurs when this happens; you get credit for all of Jesus' good stuff (perfect obedience, righteousness, right relationship) and he takes away all of your bad stuff (disobedience, sin). We are then compelled by his love to endeavor to live lives of integrity out of gratitude for what has been accomplished on our behalf.

Now that is really good news for Little Reds like us.

Come now, let us reason together, says the LORD: though your sins are like scarlet, they shall be as white as snow; though they are red like crimson, they shall become like wool.

—*Isaiah 1:18*

PARENTAL PONDERINGS

Have you ever felt that your sins were too great for God to forgive? How does knowing that Jesus came to rescue you from every sin (past, present, and future) help reconcile that feeling?

KIDS KICKSTARTS

When is the last time you disobeyed your parents? What happened? How does knowing how much Jesus loves you encourage you to do the right thing?

Part III

SACRIFICE

Chapter Seven

HANSEL AND GRETEL

Before beginning this section on sacrifice (and perhaps feeling a little convicted by the last section to be a person of integrity!), I need to admit to you that it is somewhat ironic that I am writing a book about fairy tales when a number of these tales (especially *Hansel and Gretel*) are stories that I had little to no recollection of before embarking on this project! Clearly, God has a sense of humor to call someone like me into this endeavor.

Thankfully, as it turned out, I had an excellent resource in my thirteen-year-old daughter, Katie. One afternoon when we were going for a walk around the block, I asked her if she remembered the story of Hansel and Gretel. Much to my surprise, she recounted the story in great detail (including the parts about the pebbles and breadcrumbs). She then informed me that she had neither read the story nor even thought of it since she was seven years old. But she retold this story with such clarity, as if she'd just read it yesterday. The reason I raise this point is to emphasize the importance of these stories. Many of them are ingrained in the minds and psyches of our children from their earliest years. What an incredible opportunity to, at the same deeply impressionable time in their development, also point them toward the even greater Story that all good tales point toward.

That important aside being said, I did subsequently read the story of Hansel and Gretel. I didn't need to, as it turns out that Katie's summary was spot-on.

Essentially, the story is about two siblings. They are growing up in a remote area of a great forest with their father and stepmother. Times are hard and food becomes scarce. The parents realize there is not enough food for all of them, and the stepmother persuades the father to take extreme measures by marching their children deep into the forest, where they are each given a slice of bread and abandoned. The children, however, overhear the plan, and one of them leaves a trail of pebbles on the way into the forest. After awaking in the middle of the night, afraid and alone, the kids are able to follow this trail of pebbles back home under the moonlit sky. Unfortunately, this did not lead to repentance on the part of the parents, but instead they were greeted with a rebuke from the stepmother: "You naughty children." As the story continues, the stepmother browbeats the father to proceed with the same ploy again. This time, they do not allow the children to collect pebbles, but the kids are smart enough to leave a trail of breadcrumbs. Early the next morning, when the children awaken, again alone in the dark, the parents are gone. The breadcrumbs have been devoured by the animals of the forest and they do not know how to get back home.

After wandering deep into the forest for three days, they run into a beautiful bird that leads them to a house made out of bread, cake, and sugar. Unfortunately for them, this turns out to be the house of a witch. A witch who eats children, no less! The witch proceeds to cage Hansel and forces Gretel to cook for her brother to try to fatten him up. At the climax of the story, Gretel tricks the witch and is able to push her into the furnace, lock the door behind her, and burn her up. The children are then able to make their way home, where they find their father happy to see them and their stepmother dead. The story ends, indicating "they lived together in perfect happiness."

Do you see the amazing character traits portrayed by the children in this story? They exhibit perseverance, ingenuity, bravery, and forgiveness to their father. The children express great faith and dependence on God throughout the story (e.g., "God will not forsake us," "the good God will help us," and "dear God, do help us").

If we look at the tale more closely, however, it strikes me as more of a modern-day horror film than a children's story. I mean, really, take your kids out into the forest and leave them there to die (not once but twice!). Have things go from bad to worse when they think they are rescued, but instead find a children-eating witch. And finally, go home to a father who repeatedly betrays their trust and try to live under the same roof "happily" together. Sounds more like a nightmare to me!

So how can a story like this point toward the beauty of the gospel?

Remember, there is a Father in the gospel story as well. He is a perfect Father, but he too makes a decision to send his child out to die. Oh, but this Father is very different. He loves us so deeply that he would send his Son to be a living sacrifice for us so that we might have a restored relationship with him forever.

And what about this Son, what about Jesus? He knew the plan set before him when he came to earth that first Christmas morning. The cross was the designed destination of his mission. And he was well aware of the suffering he would endure in the interim to accomplish the redemption of his people. Just like the children in the tale but much more so, he exhibited perseverance amid trials, ingenuity against deceit from one much more evil than the witch, the greatest bravery we will ever witness—and words fail me when trying to describe how amazing his forgiveness is. Jesus was completely dependent on and perfectly faithful to his Father but was forsaken on the cross . . . why? So that we would not be. The Bible says that it was "For our sake he made him [Jesus] to be sin who knew no sin, so that in him we might become the righteousness of God." (2 Corinthians 5:21)

Jesus did all this because he loves us. He loves you. He does not want the nightmare of unreconciled sin to continue. Like Hansel and Gretel, Jesus too wandered in the darkest forest imaginable for three days. After he was crucified, he descended into hell until the third day when he arose from the grave. His sacrifice for us and power over death has opened the bread-of-life-laden path back home to our Father, who welcomes us as his children with a loving embrace like no other.

Friends, that's the story I'd like to see deeply imprinted in my daughter's heart. May that be true for you and your children as well!

> So that Christ may dwell in your hearts through faith—that you, being rooted and grounded in love, may have strength to comprehend with all the saints what is the breadth and length and height and depth, and to know the love of Christ that surpasses knowledge, that you may be filled with all the fullness of God.
>
> —Ephesians 3:17–19

PARENTAL PONDERINGS

Have there been any "stepmothers" or "children-eating witches" in your life? How does knowing how much you have been forgiven change the way you respond to how you have been treated?

KIDS KICKSTARTS

Have you ever been lost like the children in the forest? When was the last time you were scared? What happened? How does it make you feel to know that you are loved by a God who is powerful, who is in control, and who promises to never leave you?

Chapter Eight

GOLDILOCKS AND THE THREE BEARS

Sacrifice can be defined as surrendering something of value for the sake of someone else. In the last chapter, one of the main themes highlighted was the sacrifice that Jesus made to accomplish our rescue. There is no one more valuable than Jesus, yet in love he sacrificed himself for our benefit. This theme is again emphasized in our next fairy tale, which is the story of Goldilocks and the Three Bears.

As the story begins, we are introduced to a young lady who goes for a walk in the forest. Finding an empty house, she knocks on the door, and when there's no answer, she decides to enter. Inside, she finds three different bowls full of porridge and tries each one of them. The first two are either too cold or too hot, but the last one is just right, and she eats it entirely up. Similarly, she tries out three different chairs. The first two are either too big or too small, but the third one is just right. Unfortunately, the chair breaks while she is sitting on it. So she moves into the bedroom, where she finds herself suddenly very sleepy. In a similar manner, she tries out each of the beds. The first two are either too soft or too hard, but the last one is just right, and she falls fast asleep. While she is sleeping, the owners of the house (three bears) return home and find their porridge eaten, one of the chairs broken, and their beds slept in. The baby bear finds Goldilocks still asleep in bed. Goldilocks awakens, screams for help, runs down the stairs and out of the house into the forest, never to return to that house again.

This is a somewhat perplexing fairy tale to me. Goldilocks must have either been amazingly brave or incredibly foolish. She is content to walk through a forest by herself, approach a house she has never seen, knock on the door, enter it without being invited in, and proceed to make herself at home. Can you imagine what you would do if someone did that in your home . . . and you found them sleeping in your bed? 911, right?

In addition, this young lady enters the domain of three bears. I don't know a lot about bears, but I do know that when they perceive that their cubs are threatened, they will protect their young. Goldilocks's response of fear and flight is completely appropriate under the circumstances. Although the story doesn't say, I suspect that the bears allowed her to go, as three bears could've easily contained and consumed a young girl sleeping in an upstairs bedroom of their home. So if I had to look for beauty in this story, I would say that it clearly lies in the kindness of the bears to let Goldilocks escape with her life.

When I think about the application of this story to life, I think about my own selfish inclinations. I want my porridge to be just right, the chair I sit in to be comfortable, and I don't want my feet to hang off my bed! Essentially, I want things my way. I want my kids to get along well. I want my wife to go to bed at a reasonable time (according to my timetable). I want coffee that I enjoy. I want my work to be less emotionally exhausting. I, I, I . . . I think I should change my name to Goldilocks!

So there is a problem here . . . me! My self-centeredness. Am I doomed to a life consumed by thinking only of myself? Thankfully, there is a way out of that dark den. Not surprisingly, I am not the solution to the problem of "me." The solution is only found in the renewal and transformation of my life through the gospel.

You see, Jesus left his home in heaven to enter the dark forest of this world. From the time of his birth, people wanted to kill him. All the male children two years old or younger in the region of Bethlehem were killed in an attempt to get Jesus. The devil tried his best to destroy Jesus, who found himself—by his own description—in the midst of "a brood of vipers," "a den of thieves," "blind guides," "hypocrites," "fools," and "whitewashed tombs." As the plot of the gospel story unfolds, we find Jesus in the garden of Gethsemane. In his humanity, he pleads with his Father to let the cup of wrath pass from him. And despite all the violence and unfaithfulness that surrounds him, his response is one of loving obedience, faithfully stating to his Father: "not my will, but yours, be done."

This kind of love is mind-boggling. Here we find a man who has done no wrong asking his dad for a reprieve from bearing the weight of the sin of humanity. Sounds like a reasonable request to me! However, as the plan for redemption required Jesus to drink the cup of wrath, he willingly accepts the will of his Father over his own. Remarkable.

This type of radical love has truly redefined the way I think about what love is. I used to think about love as being a warm feeling associated with comfort, peace, and joy. What I have come to realize is that while love may be associated with those emotions, there is always a price that has to be paid for love; love does not exist without sacrifice. Love requires that I consider the interests of someone else and put their interests first, even if that means not doing what I want to do. Love demands that life no longer be about me.

The quintessential (the best adjective in the English language would be insufficient here) example of this kind of sacrifice is exhibited by what Jesus did. He gave his life.

As I've thought about the end of the story of Goldilocks, I've thought about Jesus and how he too could have run. I have thought to myself, "Jesus, why didn't you run away from the den of bears? You are the only one who did not deserve to be mauled to death. You are the only one who lived a completely worthy life. Run away, Jesus, please run away!"

But Jesus knew his purpose. He was on a rescue mission for me and you. He knew that there would be no escape from the den of bears. The brood of vipers would envenomate him as he bore the full weight of sin on the cross, along with the wrath of his Father against that sin.

Jesus knew that I could not escape the bears. So he came to rescue me from them. Because of the sacrificial death and resurrection of Jesus, we now have hope. He gives us his Spirit so that we are able to turn away from self-centeredness and become more like his other-centeredness.

I ultimately have realized that Jesus could not run away, or I would never be rescued. And so I am left with only gratitude, amazement, and a desire to live in such a way that expresses thanks for this incredible gift that I never deserved and will never earn.

And so my prayer for myself, as well as for you, is as follows:

"Jesus, thank you. I wanted to yell to you to run away from the enemies that pursued you. But then I realized that I was that very enemy. Thank you for giving your life away so that this enemy might become your friend. Help me to live in a similar way of sacrificial love. May that love be infectious to my wife, my children, my coworkers, and my friends. And may I strive less for myself and more for the benefit of others out of gratitude for what you have done so that your name might be made great. In Jesus' name, amen."

I think I would be remiss if I did not add one last thing.

In the story of Goldilocks, she has three bowls of porridge to choose from. Jesus is not given a choice of bowls. His bowl of porridge is filled with the compost of life: apathy, betrayal, fear, anger, hopelessness, rejection, and the refuse of the unfaithfulness of humanity.

He consumes this putrid bowl of porridge in its entirety so that we will be given instead a bowl filled with his pure living water and bread of life as nourishment for our souls. It is the stark contrast of what Jesus has done for us that accentuates the amazing beauty of what we receive instead.

> *Father, if you are willing, remove this cup from me. Nevertheless, not my will, but yours, be done. And there appeared to him an angel from heaven, strengthening him.*
>
> —*Luke 22:42–43*

PARENTAL PONDERINGS

How do you define love? Do you agree
that love cannot exist without sacrifice?
How does Jesus' sacrifice on your behalf
compel you to live a life of generosity?
How have you seen God change you?

KIDS KICKSTARTS

Would you have done what Goldilocks
did? How would you have treated Goldilocks if you were one of the bears? How
does Jesus treat us for the not-so-good
things we have done? How does that make
you feel?

Chapter Nine

BEAUTY AND THE BEAST

As the story of Beauty and the Beast goes, there is a prince who is cruel and self-centered. He is visited by a witch, who subsequently casts a curse transforming him into a beast and his staff into a variety of animated objects. She pronounces that unless someone falls in love with him during a finite period of time, he and his staff will be so cursed for the remainder of their days.

The Beast is introduced to Belle, the beauty, and she sacrifices her freedom so that her father, who had been imprisoned by the Beast, can be released. They subsequently fall in love, and the Beast poignantly frees her so that she can help her father, who is in trouble.

At the climax of the story, the Beast engages in a battle with the evil Gaston, who, after stabbing the Beast, slips and falls to his death. Belle professes her love for the Beast, the curse is broken, and yes, you guessed it, they live happily ever after!

Of all of the fairy tales I've read, this is one of my favorite illustrations of the gospel because it depicts with such clarity the concepts of sacrificial love and the resultant transformation of identity. Belle willingly forfeits her freedom so that her father might be released. Subsequently, spending time with a person of such integrity ultimately begins to change the Beast as he falls in love with Belle. The corollaries here are so clear, aren't they?

In the gospel, we are presented with an even farther-reaching type of love. Our position as people who have sinned before a holy God is much worse than simply being imprisoned by a beast. The Bible has some really hard but true words to describe our unredeemed status: we are called enemies. You see, Belle sacrifices her freedom out of love for her dad, who also loves her. Similarly, the Beast risks his life out of love for Belle, who has fallen in love with him. As noble as those acts are, so much more astounding is the love of Jesus. He sacrificed his life for people who he knew would reject him, betray him, and hate him. The Bible says that while we were yet enemies, God loved us and sent his son to die for us. Let that sink in for a bit. It's like what would have happened had the Beast decided that Gaston was worth dying for and intentionally let Gaston kill him so that Gaston might one day be rescued from his completely self-absorbed way of living. This is more akin to what happens in the gospel.

In Jesus, a man who had done no wrong became the Beast of all beasts when he bore the weight of our sins on the cross . . . so horrific that his Father turned his face away. There would have to be a very powerful reason for him to do that. And there is—he loves you. Jesus willingly laid down his life in order that you and I (self-centered people very much like Gaston) might be rescued, redeemed, given new purpose, and given hope. Do you see it now? The Beauty became the Beast so that we might become his Belle.

For if while we were enemies we were reconciled to God by the death of his Son, much more, now that we are reconciled, shall we be saved by his life.
                                        —*Romans 5:10*

PARENTAL PONDERINGS

How does it make you feel that Jesus willingly became the Beast of all beasts . . . for you?

KIDS KICKSTARTS

Is it easy to be nice to someone who is mean to you? How does knowing the way Jesus has loved you help you to love others?

Part IV

FREEDOM

Chapter Ten

THE FROG PRINCE

In the story of The Frog Prince, there is a princess who loses a gold ball in a deep spring. This ball means everything to the princess, and she is distraught over having lost it. A frog appears and offers to fetch it for a price. She makes a deal with the frog that if he gets her ball, he can sleep in her bed, eat off her plate, and live in her house. Of course, as the story goes, the frog fetches the ball and, subsequently, comes every day to the princess's house. Looking for a reprieve, she goes crying to her father, who tells her that she needs to keep her promise. So she does. After three nights sleeping with the frog, the frog is transformed into a prince. We find out that he was cursed and has now been released. They get married and live happily a great many years.

On a commendable note, the father's parenting jumps out at me. He clearly values keeping one's word and becoming a person who is trustworthy over "rescuing" his daughter as she has requested. On the other hand, the daughter's response to the loss of her ball and the value she places on it are less than admirable.

When I think about the daughter's response, it reminds me of a friend's dog, Lilly, who we get to take care of every once in a while when her owners are out of town. From what I can tell, Lilly has a singular focus in life: her ball. She is relentless in her pursuit of it, unwilling to voluntarily release it, and would neglect both food and sleep to get her precious smelly, saliva-saturated squishy ball. It is what she lives for, as she is despondent and distraught without it.

It's tempting for me to poke fun at Lilly and the princess in this fairy tale. However, it does not take too much self-reflection to quickly realize that I have been similarly foolish in my own life.

I have always enjoyed video games. I grew up in the era of the Atari game system. When I was in college, I would frequently stay up into the middle of the night playing Risk on my Macintosh. As the video games became more advanced, my interest in them increased. After graduating college, I no longer had a roommate, and it became routine to stay up until 5:00 a.m. playing video games on my Sega game system. Thinking about playing video games consumed my thoughts. I was willing to sacrifice sleep, relationships, work, and food. I was addicted to video games. I was no different than Lilly; if anything, Lilly was my superior as she is consistently friendly, whereas I do not think that was true of myself in that season of my life.

The Bible has a word for these types of problems of misplaced singular focus. It's called an idol. Essentially, an idol is anything that is elevated to the place of worship. An idol demands that you give it the entirety of your attention but does not ultimately satisfy your needs and leaves you feeling empty. It can be something obvious, as in the cases described above, or it can be subtle and insidious . . . even good things like a job, a spouse, or your children can become idols in life. In my case, there was a slow drift toward idolatry. It started as a harmless pastime as a child and slowly got its hooks into me. I ultimately felt ashamed, helpless, and powerless to free myself. I did not wish to tell others of my struggles as it was embarrassing. I needed help from someone who had more willpower than me.

Thankfully, there is such a person . . . Jesus. He too had a singular focus while on Earth: to love his Father and to love others. His enemies applied constant pressure on him to shift this focus. There is no one else in human history who faced the full gamut of temptation and completed this life unblemished.

One of the times that we read about Jesus being tempted is found in the fourth chapter of Matthew. The Bible tells us that Jesus was led into the wilderness by the Spirit, where he fasted for forty days and forty nights. At the end of this time, the devil came to tempt him. Whew, talk about a time when a man would be at his weakest, right? The devil tempted him with food, authority, and riches with just one request in return . . . that Jesus would worship him. Of course, the devil didn't really have anything of substance to offer as Jesus already was in possession of everything. He is the bread of life, the King of kings and Lord of lords, and nothing can compare to the splendor of his glory. At the same time, he was fully human, and I'm sure that turning a few stones into bread after forty days of fasting was at least as tempting as getting a precious gold ball from a frog.

Jesus had a different focus, though. He knew that the road to glory would take him down a long path of suffering. The Bible has a beautiful verse that talks about what inspired him to move forward on this path: "Jesus, the founder and perfecter of our faith, who for the joy that was set before him endured the cross, despising the shame, and is seated at the right hand of the throne of God." (Hebrews 12:2) Do you have any idea what the joy was that was set before him? Was it going to heaven? Was it the seat at the right hand of the throne of God? Was it the worship he would receive? Was it the amazing food that I suspect that there has to be in heaven?

No, YOU were the joy that was set before him. He endured the suffering and the shame for you. For me. Inexplicably to my mind, he set his loving gaze on us and would not avert his eyes or change his course until he had accomplished what he had come to do: his death for our rescue, redemption, and restoration.

AMAZING.

OK, so back to me and my video game addiction. How was I rescued? I wish I could tell you that there was a three-step plan, but there was no easy formula. What I know is that our God is merciful, kind, and patient. In my case, the Scripture about gouging out your eyes or cutting off your hands if they cause you to sin resonated with me. Thankfully, I was wise enough to approach that passage nonliterally! I asked God to help free me from my slavery to video games. The best

I can understand it is that, in a beautiful way, repentance released God's mercy. By God's grace, I was able to take the video game console and throw it away in the trash can. I got to keep my eyes and hands!

The redemptive thing that God does with sin like this in our lives is to use the outcome for the benefit of others. I have much greater empathy for people trapped in recurrent patterns of sin because I get it. I understand the pull of the golden ball . . . whether toward video games, in my case, or pornography, alcoholism, gambling, masturbation—you name it.

If you happen to be someone who is where I was—broken, defeated, helpless—let me offer encouragement by reminding you that there is hope. No one is beyond rescue. Sin loves darkness and secrecy, so one of the first steps to freedom is confession. Ask God for help, then find someone who loves you and ask them to help.

It's been twenty-two years since I threw away that Sega game console, but there have been a handful of times since then that I have been sucked back into unhealthy patterns of playing video games. I have learned that I need to be wary of my weaknesses. I have employed the help of trusted friends to ask me how I am doing. (I suppose that now includes you too!) I am humbly reminded that I do not have it all together. But there is one who does have it all together, who loves me, forgives me, is with me every step of the way, and has begun a good work in my life that will continue to progress until my last breath.

May you be encouraged in your journey to remember that Jesus is more beautiful than any other object you may pursue, that he is willing to forgive you for any debt you may have, and that there is hope for a life of freedom and purpose even in the midst of the struggles and temptations of life.

> *Now to him who is able to do far more abundantly than all that we ask or think, according to the power at work within us, to him be glory in the church and in Christ Jesus throughout all generations, forever and ever. Amen.*
> —*Ephesians 3:20–21*

PARENTAL PONDERINGS

How are you like the frog prince? What are the gold balls in your life? Can you think of a time when God redeemed a sin in your life?

KIDS KICKSTARTS

How are you like the princess? What are the gold balls in your life? Have you asked God to help you let go of any gold balls before? What happened?

Chapter Eleven

PETER PAN

In the most common version of the story, Peter Pan is portrayed as heroic, noble, recklessly brave, and forever young. Tinker Bell is his trusted friend, jealous protector, and helper. She provides the magic fairy dust to help Peter and Wendy fly. As is the case in all good fairy tales, there is a gripping tension between good and evil. Captain Hook serves as the foil in this tale. At the end of the day, we see the victory of the winsomely brash Peter along with his collection of orphan friends in Neverland over the conniving foolishness of Captain Hook and his humorously inept subordinates.

Innocence, childlikeness, bravery, and freedom . . . these are beautiful traits that are highlighted in this tale. Evil is personified in such a way, however, that it seems seriously unlikely to win the day.

I'd like to highlight three things from this story.

First is the fascinating concept of the hero, Peter, who never grows up. This idea of remaining a child seems to be held up as an ideal to follow. To the contrary, one of our jobs as Christian parents is to help our children mature in ways that will allow them to successfully navigate life. In a sense, our children are guests in our home for a finite time, and we are charged with the privilege of helping shape them into independent adults.

It is important to pause for a moment to emphasize that there is a balance to be struck here. At the same time that we strive to promote this maturity, we want to encourage them to retain their childlike curiosity and faith. In fact, Jesus clearly expresses a high view of children when asked who was the greatest in the kingdom of heaven by expressing, "Truly, I say to you, unless you turn and become like children, you will never enter the kingdom of heaven." (Matthew 18:3) Accordingly, while we want them (and us parents!) to grow in childlikeness, we don't want them to remain like Peter . . . immature and perpetually childish.

Second, the story of Peter Pan is full of battle. It is another concept that is both self-evident and important to teach our kids: that life is full of conflict. My kids used to have a colossal argument about who would get to eat the "top part" of the banana. We now laugh at this, but we also use it as an example of how easy it is to make a mountain out of a molehill, especially when we all want things our way. Isn't that what Hook wants? His way in all things of value: power, control, riches, and authority. He definitely wants the top part of the banana, right? There will be many Captain Hook-type people in our lives that seem either in it for themselves or, worse, out to get us. The question for us to engage our kids with is not, "How do we change these types of people?" (which is not within our power) but "How do we respond to these situations in ways that promote the opportunity for restoration of relationship?"

Once again, the person we should be highlighting here is Jesus. He had ultimate power and authority, but in loving pursuit of us, he was willing to humble himself to the extent that he would die so that the seemingly irreconcilable conflict between us (sinful) and our Father in Heaven (sinless) could be reconciled. He literally was hooked to a cross so that we would get off the hook. Remembering the magnitude of what he has accomplished for us helps put into perspective whatever conflict we find in front of us. This is the gospel lens we want to model and help our children to wear.

Lastly (and perhaps what I have always found most intriguing and compelling) is the backstory of the clock. Hook is so named, of course, because of the absence of his left hand. Peter cut off Hook's hand in a duel and threw it into the sea, where a crocodile swallowed it along with a ticking clock. The crocodile returns throughout the story (announced in advance by the *ticktock* of the ever-running clock in his belly), striking fear into Hook.

The riveting extrapolation to me is the realization that each one of us has a "ticktock" approaching. The crocodile of death swims toward us and will eventually consume each of us. Our consolation in this is the knowledge that each day is a fragile gift from a good God who loves you, is in control, AND knows the number of your days down to the second. I recognize that this can evoke many emotional responses, but for readers who know Jesus as their only hope, I encourage you to consider that it is a call to live a life that is reflective, grateful, and purposeful by endeavoring to honor God with the gift of each day. If we are able to latch onto this truth (precious, fragile, purposeful days) and apply it in our lives, then we might also be better able to point our children toward the One who can provide a life of freedom, bravery, and heroism. I want more of that non-fairy tale reality for me and (when I am viewing life clearly through the lens of the gospel) even more so for my wife and children.

We all face the inevitability of our mortality. The emphasis we can share with conviction with our children is that we need not fear death, because Jesus has overcome the grave. He gives us purpose in this life, is committed to never leave us, and promises an eternity with him in heaven when the last tick of our clock on Earth has struck.

I have said these things to you, that in me you may have peace. In the world you will have tribulation. But take heart; I have overcome the world.
—*John 16:33*

PARENTAL PONDERINGS

When was the last time you thought about the inevitability of your mortality? How does knowing that Jesus is alive help you? When was the last time you asked God to help you live a life of freedom instead of fear?

KIDS KICKSTARTS

Do you want to remain a child forever like Peter, or do you want to grow up? Do you have a "top part of the banana" story in your home? Ask your kids what they think the purpose of parenting is (be ready with your own answer!).

Chapter Twelve

CINDERELLA

I'd like to finish this book with a chapter that depicts how gospel-centered conversations can happen in the milieu of life. As you may recall from the introduction, it was my son's prompting to "do one" that began this fairy tale journey. And as it so happened, *Cinderella* was the story my son, Bradley, chose for me to expound upon during that car ride home from church.

With a smile on my face and a shake of my head, I once again need to admit that I could not entirely remember the story of Cinderella. So I asked my son to refresh my memory. He shared with me that it is a story about a woman who lives with two mean stepsisters and a cruel stepmother. Cinderella is able to go to a big party and meet a prince, but she loses a slipper as she leaves. The prince finds her by checking everyone's foot until he finds the foot that fits the slipper. Then everyone lives happily ever after. Clearly, this was an abridged version!

"OK," I said to my son, "here goes."

The beauty in the story is exhibited in the perseverance of the woman who has been poorly treated. With the help of others, she is able to gain access to someone who can change her circumstances and rescue her.

The story goes sideways, however, when it finishes by indicating that they lived happily ever after.

I asked my son if he thought that two people were truly able to live happily ever after in a marriage, or if it is more likely that they are filled with a mixture of struggle and delight. I asked if he thought most stories ended happily, or if, in reality, he understood that many stories do not lead to rescue (homeless people, people caught in addictions, people like Cinderella who live in abusive homes). I said that we as Christians should be advocates for justice. We should be people who speak up for the poor and disenfranchised.

I also pointed out that, just like Cinderella needed to be rescued, we too need to be rescued. Our situation, however, is much more dire than Cinderella's with a few cruel family members. We face the reality of the bondage of our own sin, a devil bent on our destruction, and a holy God whose forgiveness we are not able to earn. Thankfully, we also have a much more powerful prince capable of resolving our plight. This Prince of Peace, Jesus, loved us so much that he gave us much more than a slipper to wear. He gave his very life to rescue us. He removed our sin-saturated rags and gave us his clothes of righteousness to wear instead. If we accept him as our Lord and Savior, he gives us his name, Christian, and adopts us into his family.

Because we have been liberated from sin in this way, we are free to live purposefully and passionately in gratitude for what Jesus has accomplished for us. Jesus' love, which granted our freedom, now compels us to actively engage a broken world with the compassion that we ourselves have received. And even in the midst of the frustrating ongoing struggles of life, we can be confident in the hope that one day all things will be restored. On that great day there will be no more tears, sadness, suffering, or death. In beautiful contrast, we will get to spend the rest of eternity in adoration of our Prince with a level of delight, joy, and peace that can only be imagined this side of heaven.

I think that our story of rescue is actually the most amazing Cinderella story that has ever been told.

"So how did I do, son?" I asked him.

His reply—"that's pretty good"—indicated that I had passed his "do one" challenge.

Now Joshua was standing before the angel, clothed with filthy garments. And the angel said to those who were standing before him, "Remove the filthy garments from him." And to him he said, "Behold, I have taken your iniquity away from you, and I will clothe you with pure vestments."
—Zechariah 3:3–4

PARENTAL PONDERINGS

How do you lead your family in advocating for justice? Have you experienced or witnessed a story of rescue in your life?

KIDS KICKSTARTS

Are there any children in your class at school who don't fit in or don't have many friends? How could you be a friend?

Postscript

As the cover of this book illustrates, the fairy tale characters are all trying to point you toward and lead you to the treasure. My desire in writing this book is to show you as best I can how beautiful Jesus is. He is the treasure.

While I hope that these chapters, along with the Parental Ponderings and Kids Kickstarts, will prompt many beneficial conversations, my vision for the ultimate use of this primer is much broader. I would encourage you to use this book as a template to teach your children to interpret their culture through the lens of the gospel.

For younger children, consider reading the corresponding chapter in this book before watching the movie or reading the bedtime story. Then ask the Kickstarts questions or other probing questions. What was beautiful about this story? Did anything not make sense or seem unrealistic? Then consider sharing either how the story points toward the bigger Story or providing some correctives about how it deviates from the truth. These types of questions can be asked of any bedtime story, movie, cartoon, or play. As you know, popular culture has a teaching agenda too, so it would be beneficial to your kids to equip them to navigate these issues now.

For older kids (preteens and teens), consider using the following model as a template for everything you watch together as a family.

1. Give a synopsis of the movie/sitcom/play.
2. Provide examples of how the story reveals truth and beauty.
3. With your understanding of the gospel, try to discern where it diverts from truth, and perhaps not so subtly, where it is attempting to persuade you to adopt a culturally acceptable view.

If you have multiple kids, alternate who gets to answer question 1, 2, or 3.

The hope, of course, is that our kids would develop a gospel lens through which they can discern what is right and what is deceptive. We desire for them to be equipped to be in the world, yet not of the world. To that end, my prayer for my kids and yours is that, through this book, future generations may be provided with a compass to better navigate not only fairy tales but also the vast array of secular media for their benefit and for God's glory.

Acknowledgments

We live in a community, all of us in some way, somewhere. Like you, I have benefited from the care and support of many people in my life. This is where, in the smallest of ways, I get a chance to say thank-you to them!

If you've read this book, I suspect you can guess who I'm going to thank first! The one who was willing to sacrifice his life to give me his identity, compel me to live a life of integrity, and offer a life of freedom I would never otherwise have known . . . Jesus, thank you. This book could not have been written and would have no meaning, value, or power without you.

Much gratitude to my parents, for their faithfulness to each other, and for their consistent love expressed toward me.

Thank you, Katie and Bradley, for helping me think through these fairy tales and for being such great resources to bounce ideas off of. Whether you are thirteen and ten or thirty-three and thirty, know that my love for you is resolute and passionate.

Steve, God has used you powerfully in my life to mold me, and I could not have chosen a better brother than you.

Vern, Joey, and Jeff, we have walked through many seasons of life together, and I'm so grateful for your ongoing friendship, counsel, and prayers.

Rob and Josh, thank you for reading this book at its earliest of stages and for your consistent encouragement.

I also want to recognize a few men who have had a significant impact on my thinking, although we've not met. Thank you, John Piper, Max Lucado, and Tim Keller, for your faithfulness to preaching and teaching the gospel message.

And lastly, by way of closure to this section (and also as an addendum of sorts to Chapter Two of this book), I have one very important person left to thank . . .

Like many families, we dress up in costumes on Halloween. I have been Hamilton and the Incredible Hulk in the past two years, as my costumes tend to vary. My wife, however, has worn the same costume for at least five years. She has been Snow White, which I think is a good fit for her because of her love of sleep! And while my wife is indeed beautiful when she sleeps, she exhibits consistent beauty in the way she lives that makes her truly beautiful. Gayle, your life exudes the gospel message, and I am thankful to be a part of it. I love you.

About the Author

David Swayne was raised in Southern California and educated at Duke University and Wake Forest University School of Medicine.

He loves coaching and playing football with his son. He enjoys looking up fun words with his daughter like hippopotomonstrosesquippedaliophobia (fear of long words). And he loves planning for and taking trips with his wife. He considers himself immeasurably blessed to have a wife of noble character and two amazing children.

From a vocational standpoint, David has worked for the past sixteen years as a family medicine physician. He views himself as an advocate, encourager, and counselor in partnering with his patients to live a healthy life. He has also served as an elder at church.

David lives with his family in Winston-Salem, North Carolina.

CPSIA information can be obtained
at www.ICGtesting.com
Printed in the USA
LVHW081327120819
627333LV00012B/205/P